Introduction

Most people are introduced to keeping goldfish as
pets when they buy a single Common goldfish or
receive one as a gift. Although goldfish are really
quite tough, they are completely dependent on your
skills as a petkeeper. If you take the time to learn the
basics of fishkeeping, your goldfish will be happy and
healthy and could live a long time. Goldfish kept in
good conditions have been known to live for more
than 32 years!

●*Above: A group of healthy goldfish. If living conditions
are favorable, goldfish can live for many years.*

CARING FOR
• YOUR PET •

GOLDFISH

Dr. David Sands

SMITHMARK

This edition published in 1996 by SMITHMARK Publishers, a division of U.S. Media Holdings, Inc., 16 East 32nd Street, New York, NY 10016.

1 2 3 4 5 6 7 8 9

SMITHMARK books are available for bulk purchase for sales promotion and premium use. For details write or call the manager of special sales, SMITHMARK Publishers 16 East 32nd Street, New York, NY 10016; (212) 532-6600.

ISBN 0 8317 6847 9

CREDITS

Editor: Marion Elliot **Design by:** DW Design, London
Color Separation by: Pixel Tech, Singapore
Filmset by: SX Composing Ltd., Essex
Printed in Slovenia

PICTURE CREDITS
Artists

Copyright of the artwork illustrations on the pages following the artists' names is property of Salamander Books Ltd.

Wayne Ford: 14-15, 16-17, 18-19, 34-35, 54-55, 57
Cliffford and Wendy Meadway: 28-29
Colin Newman (Linden Artists): 52-53

Photographs

The publishers wish to thank the following photographers and agencies who have supplied photographs for this book. The photographs are copyright of the photographer and have been credited by page number and position on the page: (B) bottom, (T) top, (C) centre, (BL) bottom left etc.

David Sands: 4, 7, 41, 49. Laurence E. Perkins: 6, 8
Aquila Photographics: M. Gilroy, title, 8(B), 9(T), 10(T), 10(B), 11, 12-13, 61, 63 R. Maier, 23, 51
Interpet Ltd: Bernard Bleach, 20-21, 24, 26, 27(B), 30, 31, 32-33, 36-37, 39, 42, 43, 46-47
Dick Mills: 48, 50. Heather Angell: 9(B), 10(C)
Dr. James Chubb: 59
Jacket photograph: © R. Maier, supplied by Aquila Photographics

Where goldfish come from

The many wonderful varieties of the goldfish, *Carassius auratus*, come from wild carp forms that originated in southern China. This species, developed by Chinese fish farmers over 1,000 years ago, is closely related to the Crucian carp. This fish is well known to anglers by common names such as the Golden carp.

Wild goldfish

The wild goldfish was a highly varied animal that produced unusual scaling and different colors quite naturally. As soon as people began to experiment with breeding the goldfish, all kinds of interesting colors and scales were developed. Selective breeding of wild goldfish still continues today in Japan, Europe, and North America.

Early fish breeding

The original breeding groups probably came from fish that already had unusual body shapes or interesting fins and unusual color and scales. These variations attracted the attention of fish breeders who were already breeding carp. They used their knowledge to produce unusual "golden", "long-finned" and "fantailed" forms.

Japanese fish breeders

Japanese fish breeders, who were already highly experienced at breeding the Koi carp, obtained quantities of wild and partly developed goldfish from China about 500 years ago. They used their skills to develop selective breeding programs that produced some of the most attractive varieties available today, such as the Lionhead, mirror-scaled Calico, and Shubunkin goldfish.

Domesticated goldfish

Today, there are many thousands of amateur and commercial goldfish breeders and fish farmers around the world. They have continued to selectively breed long established goldfish forms and produced the many new varieties that are available today.

Common goldfish

The best known goldfish, the Common goldfish, is not much different to the original wild form. Through selective breeding it is evenly pigmented with orange or gold. There are a number of color variations of Common goldfish, such as white and gold, and black-speckled forms.

● **Above:** *The Common goldfish is the best known of all goldfish. It has a short tail and a sturdy body with red, orange, or yellow scales.*

● **Above:** *The Comet goldfish has developed from the Common goldfish. The main difference between the two types is that the Comet has a longer tail and more pointed fins and can be a very fast swimmer.*

Comet goldfish

A further development of the Common goldfish is the elongation of fins, especially the tail fin, which can be more than three-quarters the length of the fish's body. These long-tailed types are known as Comet goldfish and are fast, graceful swimmers. Japanese goldfish breeders have produced delightful variations of the Comet tail forms including the Sarasa Comet. This goldfish has red and white bands and, like the Koi carp, has an impressive pattern when viewed from above. This form was developed for aquarists who wish to keep goldfish in an outdoor pond rather than an aquarium.

Choosing the right breed

Fancy goldfish

As well as the Common or Comet goldfish, there is also a wide range of super-fancy goldfish.

A community display of several types of goldfish, such as the Red Cap or Calico Oranda, Fantail, and the ever popular Black Moor is a wonderful sight. Goldfish are easy to dismiss as fairly commonplace animals, but finding a good quality Lionhead goldfish can prove difficult even for the most serious goldfish enthusiast!

Different forms

There are many visually stunning forms of the goldfish, including the Celestial, that has telescopic eyes positioned on top of its head, Bubble-eye, with eyes in large sacs and Ranchu, with a distinctive curved body. You will find a huge variety of colors, fin lengths and body shapes throughout the goldfish family. There are a number of color variations found in the following forms: Fantail, Oranda, Lionhead, Bubble-eye, Pompom, Pearlscale, Black Moor, Calico, and Celestial.

● *Above: Young Bubble-eye goldfish. Bubble-eyes have a large, delicate sac beneath each eye.*

● ***Right:*** *The Pompom goldfish has a threadlike development of its nostrils.*

● **Above:** *The Celestial goldfish has very striking telescopic eyes that are positioned on top of its head.*

Common fancy goldfish varieties that are suitable for aquariums

The following fancy goldfish are available in various colors, such as red and white, black and orange, all white, red, or white. There are also various tail fin formations such as Veil (drooping tail), Twin (divided tail), Fantail, and Ryukin (spread tail).

Red Cap Oranda

This goldfish has a white to yellow body and a lumpy head. It has a distinctive red area on the top of its head that gives it its name.

● **Right:** *A veiltail Red Cap Oranda goldfish with its flowing fins.*

9

Pearlscale

This goldfish is usually twintailed and has a very compact body. It has rows of distinctively raised scales with pale, pearly centers.

● *Left: The Pearlscale is a twintailed goldfish with distinctively domed scales that have a pearly center.*

Calico and Shubunkin Orandas

These goldfish have scales that may be a mixture of blue, orange, black, and white. This gives them a speckled or patchy appearance. Some have pearly scales.

● *Above: A Calico Oranda with scales in a variety of colors that give it a patchy appearance.*

Black Moor

These goldfish have black scales and bulbous, telescopic eyes. They have flowing fins and tails. They are usually twintailed.

● *Left: The Black Moor is covered in velvety-looking black scales.*

Lionhead and Ranchu

Both these forms have a distinctive curved body without a dorsal fin. The Lionhead has an orange head shaped somewhat like a raspberry.

Below: A Lionhead goldfish. Both Lionheads and Orandas have a raspberry-like growth on their heads. The Lionhead has no dorsal fin and its remaining fins are short.

Swimbladder problems

Whilst attempting to produce short-bodied goldfish forms, breeders caused a shortening of the swimbladder in some varieties. The swimbladder helps fish to maintain a balance in the water and Fantail, Lionhead and Oranda goldfish often swim awkwardly because of this development.

11

Goldfish suitable for ponds and large aquaria

Common goldfish

This is the best-known goldfish and can be yellow to deep red all over with a short tail fin. It is one of the hardiest goldfish and can live for many years.

Comet goldfish

This goldfish is orange or red with a longer tail fin than the Common goldfish. The Sarasa form is red and white.

Shubunkin (Comet and short-tailed)

These have similar bodies to the Common goldfish. They are brightly colored with red, black, white, and dark scales on a blue background.

Right: A pair of London Shubunkins. These goldfish are very similar to the Common goldfish in form but have scales in a variety of colors that give them a speckled appearance.

Understanding your goldfish

Color

The skin of a goldfish is protected by rows of scales. The scales are colored by pigment cells, known as chromatophores. Different pigment cells can combine to make colors and patterns on a fish's upper body. Scales reflect light and can also create patterns. The pigment cells in the scales change at different stages of the goldfish's development and the amount of pigment in them varies. It is this variation that sometimes causes goldfish to change color as they grow.

● *Below: A diagram showing basic goldfish anatomy.*

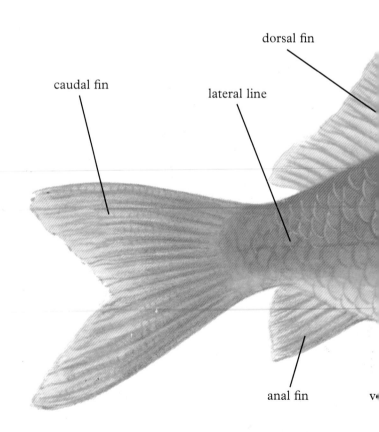

dorsal fin

caudal fin

lateral line

anal fin

v●

Swimming

Like most fish, goldfish have two sets of paired pelvic, or ventral fins and pectoral fins, together with a single dorsal, anal, and caudal fin. Their fins act as steering accessories similar to the rudder and sails of a boat. The top fin (dorsal) and the back underside fin (anal) help to keep the goldfish on line and balanced in the water. The paired fins (pelvic and pectoral), help to steer the goldfish. The tail fin (caudal), helps to drive the fish forward through the water as its body moves from side to side. This action is known as locomotion.

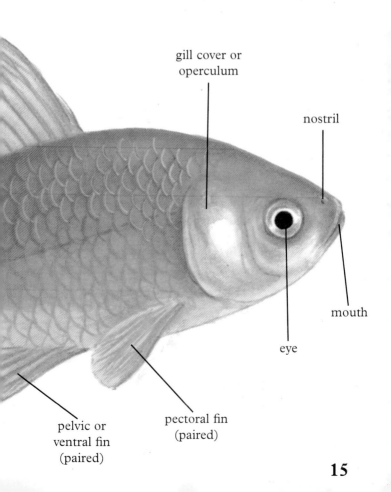

gill cover or operculum

nostril

mouth

eye

pelvic or ventral fin (paired)

pectoral fin (paired)

15

Swimbladder

All goldfish have a swimbladder. This is an internal sac that the goldfish can fill with air and gradually empty depending on water pressure. The swimbladder, together with the fins, allows the goldfish to maintain perfect balance at different depths. The swimbladder is connected by nerves to a series of inner ear bones in the fish's head and helps to amplify sound as well as aid balance.

● **Below:** *A cross-section showing the basic internal anatomy of the goldfish.*

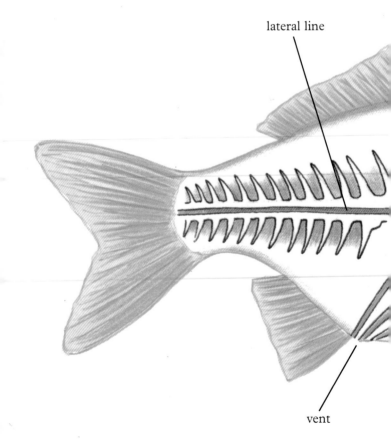

lateral line

vent

Smell and taste

Goldfish have sensory organs in their nostrils and at either side of their mouths that allow them to smell and taste. When a goldfish is hungry, it will locate a piece of food by smell, then take it into its mouth to taste it before it eats. In the wild, where visibility may be poor due, for example, to sediment in the water, a fish relies on taste and touch senses to find its food. A goldfish also uses its sensory organs to detect chemical signals in the water.

Below: The field of view of a goldfish. The goldfish is a nonpredatory fish and has eyes positioned at the sides of its head. These give it a wide angle of vision and warn it of approaching danger. The light blue area indicates low-definition sight and the dark blue, high-definition hunting sight.

Feeding

Goldfish grip food in their mouths and then use patches of fine teeth, called pharyngeal teeth, in the back of their mouths to break up and shred whatever they eat. When they have digested their food and absorbed all the goodness, they excrete the waste matter directly into the tankwater. The more your goldfish eat, the more waste matter they will produce, so you must take care not to overfeed them as this can quickly lead to severe water pollution.

Lifespan and growth

If they are kept in good conditions, goldfish can live for 20 to 30 years. In the best conditions, with regular water changes and good-quality food twice a day, a standard Common goldfish can grow to 6-8 in long. Goldfish excrete a chemical signal that controls their growth. If the chemical is not diluted by large amounts of water, growth is restricted. You must be prepared to replace your pets' tank if they outgrow the first one. All too often, goldfish are confined to unsuitably small tanks because it is felt that they are not worth the expense of a larger one.

Intelligence

Even though goldfish are not as intelligent as other pets, such as cats and dogs, they can recognize the person who feeds them and remember regular feeding times. They can also recognize objects and other fish in their enviroment.

Left: Goldfish are fairly intelligent and will eventually recognize who feeds them and remember regular feeding times.

Questions *and* Answers

My goldfish has changed color. What causes this?

Goldfish can change their color because they have special pigment cells in their skin. These make baby goldfish dark and camouflage them so that they won't be eaten. Their typical gold or orange color comes as they get older when they are more able to fend for themselves. Sickly goldfish kept in poor water conditions can sometimes lose their color as a reaction to their environment. Partial water changes can help to brighten their color. Food will also affect color. Some foods contain color-enhancing ingredients.

My goldfish opens and closes its mouth at the surface of the water. Is it hungry?

Healthy goldfish continually look for food and sometimes go up to the surface of the water to search. Don't be tempted to overfeed them though, because this can cause water pollution. Another reason could be that oxygen levels are low. It is recommended that you make a partial water change to improve the general water quality.

One of my goldfish is always chasing another one. Are they fighting?

No. It means that one of your goldfish is female and is giving out chemical signals that occur during breeding. These are being sensed by a male goldfish and he is chasing her.

How big will my goldfish grow?

This depends on the amount of space and food

available, the water temperature, and the number of water changes you make. Goldfish produce a growth chemical that controls their size. If you make lots of water changes this will dilute the chemical and allow the goldfish to grow bigger.

Does my goldfish recognize me?

Because goldfish have highly-tuned senses they can see and "feel" your presence. Over a period of time they will probably grow to recognise you.

● **Above:** Goldfish kept in good conditions with plenty of space can grow to 6-8 in long.

23

Making your goldfish comfortable

Aquariums and bowls

Goldfish are very sociable animals and thrive when kept in a community. The best home for goldfish is a 5-10 gallon bowl or a rectangular tank that is large enough to allow growth and swimming space. Small goldfish bowls are less expensive than aquariums but they don't give the goldfish much freedom. Because they have a small surface area, these bowls need careful maintenance to keep good water quality.

Size and surface area

Rectangular aquariums are better than bowls because they have a larger surface area. This means that more oxygen can enter the water from the outside. Bigger aquariums can hold a filter, a heater, a light to illuminate the water and grow plants, and ornaments, which make a much more attractive home. Because they provide more space and oxygen, aquariums usually need less maintenance than bowls.

● *Above: A rectangular aquarium or a large, 5-10 gallon bowl will make an ideal home for your goldfish.*

24

Water

Stone-cold tapwater is not good for goldfish, but you can fill a new aquarium or carry out a water change with tapwater if you use a mixture of hot and cold water and add a dechlorinator. Test the temperature of the water using an internal or stick-on thermometer before you add the fish. The ideal temperature for modern fancy goldfish is between 70°F and 75°F. Your goldfish will be more active and feed better at warmer, stable temperatures.

You could buy a compact combined heater and thermostat to keep the water at a constant temperature.

Filters

Goldfish need clean water that contains enough oxygen to allow them to breathe. Bowls and aquariums are enclosed spaces and can quickly become polluted without filtration and regular partial water changes. Fish produce waste matter, which includes a toxic substance called ammonia, directly into the water they live in. If the levels of waste get too high they can pollute the water and make your goldfish ill.

How filtration works

Water is drawn through a filter medium which traps solid particles. This is known as mechanical filtration. The filter medium also develops helpful bacteria which then go to work making fish waste safe. This is known as biological filtration. All "biological" filters work efficiently at temperatures of 70°F and upward. This is because the bacteria that they use reproduces best in warmer waters.

Alternative filter medium

Some filters also use substances such as carbon to remove toxins and keep water crystal clear, and zeolite, which removes ammonia.

The box filter

This simple, economical method for bowls and aquariums is operated by an air pump. The filter is weighted down with gravel and usually contains filter wool and carbon granules. It can also use zeolite, which absorbs the ammonia that goldfish produce.

●*Above:* The box filter is simple and economical to use. It is operated by an air pump.

Under-gravel filter

Another popular method of filtration is the under-gravel filter, which is also operated by an air pump. It is positioned below a layer of gravel. This type of filter circulates the aquarium water through the gravel where material is trapped and bacteria breaks down particles of uneaten food and fish wastes that would otherwise pollute the water. Natural colored, brown, rounded gravel, $1/16$ -$1/8$ in in diameter, at a maximum depth of 1 in, is recommended for use with an under-gravel filter.

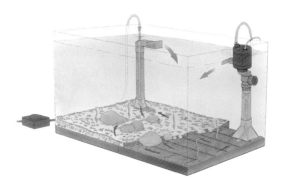

● *Above:* Under-gravel filters circulate tankwater through the gravelbed where bacteria breaks down waste matter.

Power filters

The third method of filtration, which is the best but also the most expensive, is the power filter. The internal power filter acts in the same way as the box filter but is driven by its own impeller motor rather than an external air pump. Internal power filters usually contain sponge filter medium but some can also contain carbon. The external power filter is a canister which is placed outside the aquarium. It has an intake and an outlet pipe connecting it with the aquarium. All the water is drawn out of the tank by gravity, passed through a wide variety of filter media inside the canister, and then pumped back into the aquarium.

The filter medium in both types of power filter needs to be rinsed in a bucket of aquarium water either weekly or monthly depending on the type and size of tank and the number of fish in it.

● *Right:* These internal power filters are driven by electric motors.

Oxygen

Goldfish are aerobic. This means that they need oxygen in their water to live. The amount of oxygen found in the water depends on several things including the temperature and circulation of the water and the surface area of the aquarium or bowl. The cooler the water, the more oxygen it contains, so it is important not to let the water get too warm. Circulating the water encourages more oxygen uptake.

Stocking levels

What matters when stocking a bowl or an aquarium is the amount of surface area it has. For example, a narrow-necked container that holds as much water as a wide-necked container can support fewer fish because it has a smaller surface area and less oxygen can enter the water. The ideal amount of space for each fish is 1in of fish, excluding tail, for every 30 square inches of surface area.

A ten gallon tank with a large surface area will comfortably support 3 to 4 fish providing there is good filtration and plenty of partial water changes. You should not keep more than one fish in a bowl.

● **Below:** *The surface area of your tank will determine how many goldfish it can support. A small bowl is suitable for one goldfish. The water level should be kept to the widest part of the bowl to maximize surface area. Although both the tanks shown here hold the same volume of water, the one with the larger opening can support more goldfish because more oxygen can enter the water.*

Decoration

The aquarium or bowl should be decorated to give
your goldfish the best possible home. It may contain
plants (both live and artificial), rocks, pebbles, and
ornaments. There is a variety of ornaments available
including divers, bridges, and sunken castles. Some
ornaments are action models that are operated by an
air pump. These are fun to use and also help
circulate the water. It is best to buy ornaments from
a good aquatic dealer or pet supplies store. Some
plastic and metal items are poisonous and can
pollute the water.

● **Above:** *Air-pump ornaments look attractive in an
aquarium and also circulate the water.*

Gravel and sand

There is a wide range of gravels and sands available.
These include colored gravels ranging from black to
bright red and natural colored gravel and sand. Put
new gravel or sand in a clean bucket and rinse it
thoroughly in tapwater to remove all dust and dirt
before you add it to your aquarium. Water-worn rocks
can also be added to your goldfish's home but avoid

limestone and calcium because they can affect the chemical balance of the water. You could back your aquarium or bowl with a picture scene or colored cardboard to make it decorative and give your fish some cover.

Lighting

Bowls and small aquariums do not need lighting. Larger aquariums should be illuminated by fluorescent tube lighting for ten hours a day if the tank contains live aquatic plants. Otherwise, the light should only be on during the evening, as too much light will stimulate the growth of green algae. There is a variety of fluorescent tubes available and some will even enhance the color of your fish and aquarium. An aquatic dealer will advise you on the type of light you need according to the size and depth of your aquarium.

● **Below:** *A fluorescent tube can be used in the aquarium making it more attractive and the fish easier to see.*

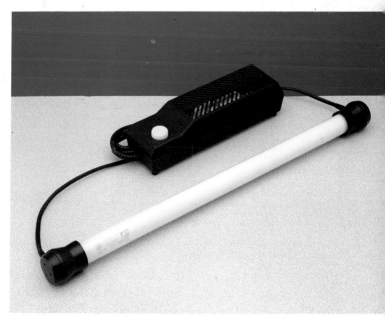

Plants

If there is a deep enough layer of gravel or sand and lighting is provided, it is possible to grow live plants in your goldfish's home. Goldfish enjoy eating live plants but they tend to dig up the roots as they forage for food. You can prevent this by using potted plants. Placing a few small pebbles around the base of each plant will keep it weighted down. It is possible to reduce your goldfish's desire to eat plants by adding foods such as peas and finely chopped greens to its diet. Some plants have tough leaves that cannot be eaten by goldfish. Java Fern and Indian

Fern are ideal plants for the coldwater aquarium because they are not edible. The common oxygenating plant, Elodea, is also ideal. Fine-leafed plants are an attractive addition and will thrive in a well-lit, clean aquarium, but their soft leaves are very appetizing to hungry goldfish! Most aquatic retailers stock a wide range of artificial plants which are modeled on the real thing and look just like live aquarium plants.

● **Below:** *Artificial plants look just like the real thing but they cannot be eaten by hungry goldfish!*

Positioning goldfish bowls

A goldfish bowl is fairly lightweight when filled and can be placed almost anywhere in the home. Avoid a window space as excessive heat and light will cause green algae blooms, which can pollute the water with fatal consequences. Worktops or hall tables are ideal as long as they are away from electrical appliances, noise, excessive movement, and direct sunlight.

●**Below:** *Strong sunlight, cooking smells, noise, and vibration all make this an unsuitable site for an aquarium.*

Positioning aquariums

A fully filled aquarium is very heavy and must be placed on an extremely secure structure or a strong stand that can be fixed firmly to a wall. The aquarium should be placed in a shady, central spot where all the family can enjoy it. Stand it near an electrical outlet for convenience. It is best to avoid areas where there will be excessive cooking smells, movement, or noise which will stress the fish. It is worth siting the tank near a tap to make partial water changes easier.

Buying a goldfish

It is best to buy your goldfish from a good aquatic dealer or pet supplies store. When you arrive, check that all the aquariums are clean and that the goldfish do not show any signs of damaged fins or scales, or red blotches on their bodies. When your goldfish have been caught and placed in a water-filled plastic bag, put them in a shopping bag to shade them from excessive light during the journey home.

● *Below:* New fish should be introduced to the temperature of an aquarium by floating the bag on the water's surface for 20 minutes.

Introducing new fish

Before you add new fish to your aquarium you should open their bag and pour some aquarium water into it. This will allow temperatures and water conditions to equalise. After 10-15 minutes, release the fish into the aquarium. Let them get used to their new conditions before you feed them. Offer each fish a couple of flakes of food after 4-5 hours and then wait until the next day before feeding them again.

Starting a new goldfish home

Many fishkeepers experience problems in the first few weeks of the life of a new goldfish home. This is

because the bacteria that breaks down fish waste takes 6-8 weeks to develop, so water quality is often a problem. To reduce problems for the first four weeks, stock only one goldfish and carry out a 30% water change every other day. Keep a constant level of one teaspoon of tonic salt per gallon of water. You can also add a biostart product.

Increasing stocks

After 4 weeks, build up to full stock level by adding one new fish to the tank every 4 weeks. Care kits for new aquariums are available and these help to establish a problem-free environment.

Questions *and* Answers

What is the best home for my goldfish?
Goldfish are tough and will survive in small glass bowls but they are happiest in a large, wide-necked bowl or aquarium. You will need to buy a tank that holds at least five gallons of water to house two goldfish comfortably.

How do I keep the water clean?
You should make a partial water change to the aquarium once a week. Stir up the gravel before changing the water so that you can remove as much sediment as possible. Filters will also help keep the water clean.

The aquarium water goes green. Why does this happen?
If the water turns green this is a sign that it is full of algae. This is usually caused by strong light, which stimulates the algae to grow. Move your aquarium to a shadier spot and make a partial water change to remove the nutrients on which the algae thrive.

What is the best position for my goldfish bowl or aquarium?
It is important to place your goldfish bowl or aquarium out of direct light in a shady part of the room. Avoid excessive heat, light, noise, vibration, and electrical appliances.

Do I need to put ornaments in my goldfish's bowl or tank?
By including aquarium ornaments you are making your fish's home more interesting. Some

ornaments are designed to be connected to an air pump and so will help circulate and aerate the water.

Does my tank need a filter?

Using a filter helps to maintain good water quality in an aquarium and make fish waste harmless. If goldfish bowls can be partially water-changed regularly they are less likely than aquariums to need filtration.

● **Above:** Ornaments will make your goldfish's home more interesting. Some help circulate the water.

Looking after bowls and aquariums

The best way to keep your goldfish healthy is to give them regular care and attention. If you provide good filtration, a stable and reasonable temperature range (70°F-75°F), a bunch of oxygenating plants, a balanced diet, and regular partial water changes, they will thrive and grow.

Water changes

Active, well-fed goldfish will soon pollute their home. Clean, fresh water is "fresh air" to your goldfish, so partial water changes must be made regularly to prevent fish wastes from building up and harming your pets. A mixture of warm and cold water with a dechlorinator will provide the right water change. You should never change the aquarium water completely. Sudden changes in a fish's surroundings can be very harmful.

● **Left:** *A syphon gravel cleaner is used to remove sediment from the gravel.*

Frequency of changes

The correct number of water changes and their frequency depends on how many fish you have and the size of their aquarium or bowl. As a rough guide, you should change about 30% of the total water every week. If the aquarium contains gravel, stir it up before changing the water. At least every two weeks use a syphon gravel cleaner to remove sediment from the gravel otherwise it will build up and affect the water quality.

Algae

Excessive green algae on the aquarium glass or in the water could mean that the tank is getting too much light. The chemical balance of the water may also have changed, which happens when the goldfish have outgrown their aquarium, or are being overfed. If algae is a nuisance (a little bit is beneficial), move the tank out of direct sunlight and only have aquarium lighting on during the evening. You could also increase the size of the partial water changes so long as a dechlorinator and a mixture of hot and cold tapwater are used.

● **Above:** *A goldfish in poor water conditions. Partial water changes should be made regularly to prevent a build-up of fish waste and sediment.*

Filters

Internal box or power filters should have their contents rinsed in aquarium water every two to four weeks depending on the number of fish you have. Remove some water directly from the aquarium for this purpose. If you rinse filter medium under the tap, chlorine can destroy the essential bacteria that is needed to maintain water quality. If carbon or zeolite are used in the filter they should be replaced every two months.

●*Above:* Use aquarium water to rinse trapped dirt particles out of the filter sponge.

Filter maintenance

It is important to check your filter, pump, and water quality every day. If any equipment breaks down it should be repaired or replaced as soon as possible to avoid causing stress to your goldfish. You can check that your filter is working with a simple kit that tests for nitrite. If there is no nitrite present in the water, the filter is working properly.

Feeding your goldfish

Goldfish will eat everything that they can find, so you must make sure that you do not overfeed them. The ideal goldfish food should contain carbohydrates and fats for energy, proteins for growth and vitamins for health and tissue repair. Most good quality flake and pellet foods contain the correct balance of these essential ingredients.

● *Above:* Various types of goldfish food:
  (1) Freeze-dried krill;
  (2) Flake food;
  (3) Freeze-dried Daphnia;
  (4) Hoops of goldfish health food;
  (5) Freeze-dried raw shrimp;
  (6) Freeze-dried Tubifex worms;
  (7) Freeze-dried Bloodworms;
  (8) Frozen Daphnia;
  (9) Frozen Bloodworms.

Giving a balanced diet

As well as the basic diet of a few whole flakes or pellets of food per fish, twice a day, you can supplement your goldfish's meals with treats such as frozen and freeze-dried foods, or even peas and a small amount of shredded shrimp twice a week.

Avoiding overfeeding

It is very important not to overfeed your goldfish. Uneaten food that falls to the bottom of the tank will start to decay and will quickly pollute the aquarium water. This may cause health problems for your pets.

Working out a rota system

Unless you work out a weekly rota system for feeding your goldfish, each member of your family may be tempted to sprinkle a few flakes of food into the aquarium every time they pass. If you share the aquarium with a brother or sister, one of you should be responsible for feeding and water changes one week and the other the next.

Varying the diet

It is important to vary your goldfishes food so that they get a balanced diet. Although goldfish enjoy live foods such as Daphnia and Tubifex worms, live foods can cause health problems. Any parasites and bacterial infections that the live foods contain could be passed on to your goldfish.

Frozen and freeze-dried foods

There is a wide range of preserved frozen and freeze-dried foods available from aquatic dealers. These include zooplankton shrimp, Tubifex worms, Daphnia and Bloodworms. These foods are safe when frozen, because the process of freezing prevents them introducing diseases into your aquarium or bowl.

Questions *and* Answers

How much should I feed my aquarium goldfish?
Aquarium goldfish only need small amounts of food. Each goldfish should be fed two or three whole pellets or flakes of fish food twice a day.

Should I give my goldfish live food?
Live Daphnia, Cyclops or Bloodworms could carry parasites that will harm your fish. It is best to vary their diet with small quantities of preserved frozen or freeze-dried foods or frozen peas.

Why does my goldfish eat the plants?
Plants and green algae are part of the natural diet of all goldfish. They enjoy eating fresh oxygenating plants and these should be provided along with green foods such as washed peas and softened green beans.

Is there any extra treat that I can give my goldfish?
Small amounts of frozen, freeze-dried or preserved foods, shredded shrimp, tiny earthworms or a few peas are all the treats that a goldfish needs. Pellets and flaked food contain all the essential daily minerals and vitamins that a goldfish needs.

How can I make sure that my goldfish are not overfed?
Organise a rota system so that everyone in your family is responsible for feeding your goldfish and making water changes on set days. This will prevent overfeeding and water pollution.

Handling your goldfish

If you need to move your goldfish to another
container, they should be gently netted rather than
moved by hand. Goldfish are cold blooded animals
and are uncomfortable when they are handled by
warm blooded humans. Rough handling can also
damage a goldfish's protective body mucus and cause
bacterial infections.

● **Below:** *Use a fine mesh net to catch your goldfish if you
need to move them. Don't touch their bodies with your
hands or you could damage their protective covering.*

Using a net

When you move your goldfish, use a soft, fine mesh net and gently catch the fish. Rest the net at the surface, keeping the goldfish in the water until you are ready to transfer it to the new location. If the new aquarium is some distance away, have a small plastic bowl filled with some of the old aquarium water ready to carry the goldfish to its new destination. If the goldfish is kept in a large aquarium, it is best to use two nets, one to guide the fish toward the surface and the other to capture it.

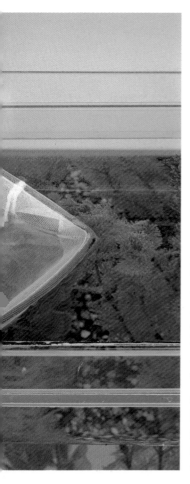

Avoiding temperature changes

When transferring goldfish between waters you must take care to avoid moving them between very different temperatures and water chemistry, as such changes can easily cause a great deal of stress.

Preparation of the new environment

To keep both water temperatures and chemistry as similar as possible it is a good idea to mix the two different waters 50/50 beforehand. When the temperatures and water chemistry have equalized, your goldfish can be gently released into their new environment.

Breeding goldfish and caring for the young

Goldfish are extremely social animals and they thrive when kept in groups. They naturally shoal, forage and feed in groups and are likely to reproduce when kept together.

Males and females

You can tell a female from a male goldfish in a breeding pair quite easily. The male is usually smaller and more slender than the female and in the breeding season has white prickles on its gill covers.

● **Above:** *A male Bristol Shubunkin with white prickles on its gill covers, indicating that it is in the breeding season.*

Spawning

Although it is not aggressive, a male goldfish will continually chase a female around the aquarium during the spawning season, which stimulates the female goldfish to release her tiny eggs for the male to fertilize.

The breeding tank

Once spawning has happened, remove the parents and hatch out the young in a separate aquarium. Fill the aquarium with 50% aquarium water and 50% fresh water. Add bunches of oxygenating plants such as Elodea and position the tank in a shady corner, preferably in a shed or garage. You can buy various fry foods for young fish from your aquatic dealer or pet supplies store. These range from liquid foods suitable for the first few weeks of life, to powdered flake food.

The young goldfish

Very young goldfish (fry) are often dark brown or black because they need to be camouflaged for the first few months to save them from being eaten. Their golden color develops after several months. Once the fry measure around 1 in long, they can be safely put back into the aquarium.

● **Below:** *Goldfish fry in a separate aquarium. They have brown or black scales when very young.*

Mixing with other fish

Coldwater aquarium displays can be made even more interesting by adding other fish such as Weather Loaches. These will thrive on peas, shredded shrimp, and most pellets and food flakes. Some of the more unusual coldwater fish, such as the European Bitterling and the North American Red-nosed Dace are seasonally available from good aquatic dealers. They are attractive additions to medium and large aquariums. Most fancy goldfish will thrive in coldwater and tropical aquariums, provided that aggressive or territorial fish are not present.

● *Left: The European Bitterling is one example of a fish that will live harmoniously with goldfish.*

Aggressive fish

Some North American freshwater species can be aggressive toward goldfish, especially the Madtoms, Bullhead or Channel catfishes. These are brown to white (albino) catfish that are sometimes available as youngsters and can be identified by their whiskers. They can measure from 4 in to 28 in when fully grown. North American catfish have sharp spines and they are nocturnal (active at night) and aggressively territorial. In the wild, they would feed on young fish, shrimps, and any small creatures that fall into the water. In an aquarium, these catfish grow fairly large and can be too robust for even the largest goldfish. Some perch-like Sunbass species can also be aggressive and all but the pygmy species should be avoided.

Going on vacation

If your goldfish are healthy and are kept in an
aquarium with good water quality, they can safely be
left for at least a week without a daily feed. It would
be a good idea to add a fresh bunch of oxygenating
plants to the aquarium before you leave, to give your
goldfish something to nibble on. You can buy
slow-release food blocks, but overuse can affect water
chemistry and quality. If you have to leave your
goldfish for longer than one week, it is a good idea to
ask a relative or neighbor to feed them two or three
times a week. If this isn't possible, there are various
battery-operated automatic feeders available at
aquatic dealers which release set amounts of food
into the water every day. Most goldfish are overfed
anyway and a short period without food will do them
no harm, providing that you make a partial water
change before going on vacation.

● **Below:** *A fresh bunch of plants will give your goldfish
something to nibble on while you are away on vacation.*

Goldfish healthcare

How to tell if your goldfish is sick

If your goldfish starts to behave differently from normal or there is a change in its appearance, it may be suffering from an infection. There are several common goldfish diseases and each has its own recognizable "signs" or symptoms.

Common infections

Scale damage, red blotches on the body, shredded or rotted fins, white growths around the mouth or clamping the fins close to the body are all signs of infection in goldfish. You can buy medicines to treat common ailments from an aquatic retailer or pet supplies store. Most medicines work best if you partially change the aquarium water first.

● **Below:** *This diagram shows the signs, or symptoms, of some of the most common goldfish diseases.*

Dropsy: The goldfish's scales protrude due to accumulated fluid.

Treatments

Add a tablespoon of tonic or aquarium salt per gallon of aquarium water (dissolved first in a pint of warm water) to the tank at the same time as the medicine as this supports the treatment. If your goldfish are showing signs of an infection but you don't know what it is or how to treat it, visit your aquatic retailer's or pet supplies store. Most will have a selection of remedies and water-testing aids as well as someone who can offer you advice.

White spot:
...y white
...ots.

Cloudy eye: This appears as a white film over the eye.

Skin flukes: burrow below the fish's skin.

Mouth fungus: a white growth around the mouth.

Gill flukes: These attach themselves to the fish's gill and may cause gasping and 'flashing'.

53

Caring for sick fish

Because goldfish are generally kept at low temperatures, all medicines take quite a long time to work. Allow at least ten days for partial recovery and feed ill fish very sparingly and carefully during the period of treatment. Sick aquarium fish are best kept in their own tank rather than a separate one. If one fish has an infection, then it is likely that all the fish will eventually get it. Removing a fish from its usual environment will also stress it unnecessarily.

Poor water conditions

If your goldfish start itching, (rubbing their bodies against gravel), flashing, (rising to the surface and sometimes partially jumping out of the water), or gasping, the water quality may be poor. To remedy the situation, make a large partial water change using a mixture of dechlorinated hot and cold tapwater. It is important to stir up any sediment that has built up in the floor covering and syphon or dump it with the old water. If your fish continue to itch, they are probably suffering from a parasite infection which needs treating with a proprietary remedy.

Swimbladder disease

One side-effect of the intensive breeding that produced short-bodied goldfish such as Red Cap Orandas is a shortened swimbladder. At the first sign of disease or poor water quality, these fish will begin to lose their balance. To treat this problem, make a partial water change (up to 50%) using hot, dechlorinated tapwater. Fit a heater thermostat to the aquarium and keep the water at a constant temperature of 70°F-75°F.

Add tonic salt to the water and treat your fish with an anti-internal bacteria product. Varying the diet to include finely shredded shrimp and soft peas should also help. To maintain good water quality, have only a thin scattering of gravel on the bottom of the tank and filter the water with an internal or external power filter.

● **Left:** *If you notice your goldfish gasping at the surface of the aquarium, poor water quality may be to blame. A large partial water change should improve conditions.*

CHECKLIST – Recognizing common goldfish infections

BACTERIAL

- Fin rot: Visual signs are splitting and reduction or complete loss of fins. Also shows as redness in the fins.

- Fungus: A white growth around the mouth, eyes, or body.

- Ulcers: Body damage. Shows as a dented red sore on the body.

PARASITIC

- White spot: Fine, white, dusty spots especially visible on the fins.

- Gill flukes: These are not often visible, but a sign that your goldfish may be carrying them is if it gasps and "flashes" excessively.

- Leeches: Dark, segmented, wormlike creatures that may be seen attached to a fish's body.

- Fish lice: Small, circular creatures about the size of a drawing pin head. They are often transparent and attach themselves to fishes bodies.

- Microscopic protozoan and fluke parasites: Slimy white skin.
A white film over the lens of the eye.

Going to the vet

When to take your goldfish to the vet
If your goldfish shows signs of a serious infection such as a tumor (appearing as a lump on the outside of its body, or a swelling inside its body), an ulcer, or severe fin or body rot, take it to your vet for examination. Your vet can prescribe antibiotic treatments for extreme cases. Less serious infections and parasite infestations can be treated in the aquarium with medicines from your aquatic dealer.

Transporting your goldfish
The best way to transport your goldfish to the vet is in a sealable plastic fish bowl or in a special polythene fish bag. Fill the bowl or bag with a 50/50 mix of fresh tapwater and aquarium water and place it in a wide shopping bag to shade your goldfish from direct light during its journey.

● ***Below:*** *Shade your goldfish from direct light during its journey to and from the vet.*

Questions *and* Answers

My goldfish holds its fins close to its body and swims awkwardly. Is this a disease?
This behavior is known as "fin clamping" and is often a sign that the fish is ill or that the water quality is poor because of fish wastes, such as ammonia. It is best to make a 50% partial water change and add a disease treatment to the bowl or aquarium.

My goldfish has white on its mouth. What does this mean and how should I treat it?
This means that your goldfish has a bacterial infection called mouth fungus. This suggests that the water quality is poor or that uneaten food is polluting the aquarium. Make a 50% partial water change and add a mouth fungus or bacterial infection remedy to the water that is used to refill the bowl or aquarium. The remedy instructions should be followed carefully.

My fish scratches itself on the gravel and ornaments. What causes this?
There are two possible reasons. The aquarium water may have been polluted by fish wastes and uneaten food. Alternatively, you may have introduced parasites into the aquarium if you have recently added more fish. Whichever the reason, you should treat the problem immediately. Make a partial water change and add a parasitic remedy. The remedy instructions should be followed carefully.

My goldfish has difficulty swimming and sometimes floats up to the surface. What shall I do?

Your goldfish is suffering from swimbladder disease which is an infection that seems to affect the inside of the goldfish. Make a partial water change and add an anti-internal bacteria remedy and tonic salt to the water that is used to refill the bowl or aquarium. Try to keep the water at a constant temperature (use a heater thermostat if necessary).

My goldfish has split fins and they are being eaten away. What causes this and how do I treat it?

The loss of fins is known as fin rot. This is a bacterial infection caused by poor water quality. Stir up the gravel and make a 50% partial water change. Add some tonic salt (one teaspoon per gallon of water) and fin rot remedy to the aquarium or goldfish bowl.

● ***Above:*** *A goldfish displaying signs of extreme tail and fin rot, which is caused by a bacterial infection.*

CARE CHECKLIST

DAILY CHECKLIST
Bowls and Aquariums:
- Goldfish need to be fed two pellets or flakes each twice a day (including varying the diet with other treats).
- Check that air pumps and filters are working properly if you have them.
- Observe the fish to ensure that they are happy and free from disease.

WEEKLY CHECKLIST
Aquariums:
- Make a partial water change of up to 30%.
- Clean algae off the front of the aquarium glass and remove dead leaves from aquatic plants.
- Rinse internal power filters in aquarium water.

Bowls:
- At the start of the week, remove half the old, stale water. Clean algae off the glass and rinse the filter in bowl water. Prepare fresh tapwater in a separate bowl. Match the temperature of the old water with hot and cold tapwater and add a dechlorinator. Refill the bowl.
- Midweek, add a product to the bowl to get rid of harmful waste, freshen water, and act as a tonic to the goldfish.

MONTHLY CHECKLIST
Aquariums:
- Make a partial water change and stir up the sand or gravel to syphon off any sediment. Ideally, use a gravel cleaner.
- Replace carbon or zeolite in filters every other month.
- Rinse filter media in aquarium water.

Bowls:

● Place goldfish in a mug or bowl and cover it to stop the fish from jumping out.

● Stir up gravel and wipe over glass using stale water. Tip the water away. Refill the bowl with tapwater of the same temperature as the old water. Treat with dechlorinator, stir, and allow to settle. Return your fish to the bowl.

● *Above:* Keep your goldfish healthy and happy with a daily, weekly, and monthly care regime.

61

About my goldfish

MY GOLDFISH'S NAME IS

_____

WHAT TYPE? MY GOLDFISH IS A

_____

Stick a photo of your pet here

MY GOLDFISH'S FAVORITE PLANT IS

_____

MY GOLDFISH'S FAVORITE FOOD IS

_____

_____

MY VET'S NAME IS

_____

MY VET'S TELEPHONE NUMBER IS

_____

Index